# SOME MAJOR EVENTS IN WORLD WAR II

## THE EUROPEAN THEATER

**1939** SEPTEMBER—Germany invades Poland; Great Britain, France, Australia, & New Zealand declare war on Germany; Battle of the Atlantic begins. NOVEMBER—Russia invades Finland.

**1940** APRIL—Germany invades Denmark & Norway. MAY—Germany invades Belgium, Luxembourg, & The Netherlands; British forces retreat to Dunkirk and escape to England. JUNE—Italy declares war on Britain & France; France surrenders to Germany. JULY—Battle of Britain begins. SEPTEMBER—Italy invades Egypt; Germany, Italy, & Japan form the Axis countries. OCTOBER—Italy invades Greece. NOVEMBER—Battle of Britain over. DECEMBER—Britain attacks Italy in North Africa.

**1941** JANUARY—Allies take Tobruk. FEBRUARY—Rommel arrives at Tripoli. APRIL—Germany invades Greece & Yugoslavia. JUNE—Allies are in Syria; Germany invades Russia. JULY—Russia joins Allies. AUGUST—Germans capture Kiev. OCTOBER—Germany reaches Moscow. DECEMBER—Germans retreat from Moscow; Japan attacks Pearl Harbor; United States enters war against Axis nations.

**1942** MAY—first British bomber attack on Cologne. JUNE—Germans take Tobruk. SEPTEMBER—Battle of Stalingrad begins. OCTOBER—Battle of El Alamein begins. NOVEMBER—Allies recapture Tobruk; Russians counterattack at Stalingrad.

**1943** JANUARY—Allies take Tripoli. FEBRUARY—German troops at Stalingrad surrender. APRIL—revolt of Warsaw Ghetto Jews begins. MAY—German and Italian resistance in North Africa is over; their troops surrender in Tunisia; Warsaw Ghetto revolt is put down by Germany. JULY—allies invade Sicily; Mussolini put in prison. SEPTEMBER—Allies land in Italy; Italians surrender; Germans occupy Rome; Mussolini rescued by Germany. OCTOBER—Allies capture Naples; Italy declares war on Germany. NOVEMBER—Russians recapture Kiev.

**1944** JANUARY—Allies land at Anzio. JUNE—Rome falls to Allies; Allies land in Normandy (D-Day). JULY—assassination attempt on Hitler fails. AUGUST—Allies land in southern France. SEPTEMBER—Brussels freed. OCTOBER—Athens liberated. DECEMBER—Battle of the Bulge.

**1945** JANUARY—Russians free Warsaw. FEBRUARY—Dresden bombed. APRIL—Americans take Belsen and Buchenwald concentration camps; Russians free Vienna; Russians take over Berlin; Mussolini killed; Hitler commits suicide. MAY—Germany surrenders; Goering captured.

## THE PACIFIC THEATER

**1940** SEPTEMBER—Japan joins Axis nations Germany & Italy.

**1941** APRIL—Russia & Japan sign neutrality pact. DECEMBER—Japanese launch attacks against Pearl Harbor, Hong Kong, the Philippines, & Malaya; United States and Allied nations declare war on Japan; China declares war on Japan, Germany, & Italy; Japan takes over Guam, Wake Island, & Hong Kong; Japan attacks Burma.

**1942** JANUARY—Japan takes over Manila; Japan invades Dutch East Indies. FEBRUARY—Japan takes over Singapore; Battle of the Java Sea. APRIL—Japanese overrun Bataan. MAY—Japan takes Mandalay; Allied forces in Philippines surrender to Japan; Japan takes Corregidor; Battle of the Coral Sea. JUNE—Battle of Midway; Japan occupies Aleutian Islands. AUGUST—United States invades Guadalcanal in the Solomon Islands.

**1943** FEBRUARY—Guadalcanal taken by U.S. Marines. MARCH—Japanese begin to retreat in China. APRIL—Yamamoto shot down by U.S. Air Force. MAY—U.S. troops take Aleutian Islands back from Japan. JUNE—Allied troops land in New Guinea. NOVEMBER—U.S. Marines invade Bougainville & Tarawa.

**1944** FEBRUARY—Truk liberated. JUNE—Saipan attacked by United States. JULY—battle for Guam begins. OCTOBER—U.S. troops invade Philippines; Battle of Leyte Gulf won by Allies.

**1945** JANUARY—Luzon taken; Burma Road won back. MARCH—Iwo Jima freed. APRIL—Okinawa attacked by U.S. troops; President Franklin Roosevelt dies; Harry S. Truman becomes president. JUNE—United States takes Okinawa. AUGUST—atomic bomb dropped on Hiroshima; Russia declares war on Japan; atomic bomb dropped on Nagasaki. SEPTEMBER—Japan surrenders.

**WORLD AT WAR**

# Fall of the Fox: Rommel

# WORLD AT WAR

# Fall of the Fox: Rommel

By G.C. Skipper

CHILDRENS PRESS, CHICAGO

Rolling sands of the North African desert

*For Stephen B. Haas, with special thanks for his 'technical'*
*knowledge, his sense of history, and—more importantly—his friendship*

**FRONTISPIECE:**
Sketch of Rommel

Library of Congress Cataloging in Publication Data

Skipper, G.C.
   The fall of the fox, Rommel.

   (His World at war)
   SUMMARY: Describes the events that turned
victory to defeat for the German troops in North
Africa led by Field Marshal Rommel during World War II.
   1. World War, 1939-1945—Campaigns—Africa,
North—Juvenile literature. 2. Rommel, Erwin,
1891-1944—Juvenile literature. [1. World War,
1939-1945—Campaigns—Africa, North. 2. Rommel,
Erwin, 1891-1944] I. Title. II. Series.
D766.82.S48     940.54'23     80-17191
ISBN 0-516-04785-X

**PROJECT EDITOR:**
Joan Downing

**CREATIVE DIRECTOR:**
Margrit Fiddle

## PICTURE CREDITS:
NATIONAL ARCHIVES: Cover, pages 6, 9
(bottom), 10, 11 (left and bottom right),
13, 15, 17, 18, 19, 22 (left), 23, 27 (left),
29, 34, 37, 38, 40, 43, 46
U.S. ARMY PHOTOGRAPH: pages 4, 9
(top), 11 (top right), 24, 26, 27 (right),
30, 45
UPI: pages 22 (right), 33
U.S. AIR FORCE PHOTO: pages 32, 41, 44
LEN MEENTS: pages 20-21 (map)

## COVER PHOTO:
Field Marshal Erwin Rommel
examines a campaign map

The North African desert stretched out before him. Its sand rolled like a great tobacco-colored dry wave. It dipped beyond vision into the horizon. General Erwin Rommel, one of the most famous military leaders of World War II, removed his cap and wiped the sweat from his brow.

He watched his men moving listlessly under the harsh, bright sun. For a brief moment he wished it were night. At least, he thought, the attacks from the British had eased up. If only the sun would do the same. But it was foolish to wish for night. The desert would grow bitterly cold once the sun was gone. Darkness would bring a different kind of discomfort to his men. At times he did not know which was worse.

"Are you feeling any better, General?" an aide asked.

Rommel replaced his cap and turned back to the map he had spread out on a table. "I'll be all right. It's just an infection." This was no time to discuss personal problems.

To change the conversation Rommel asked, "Is there any news from the supply convoy?"

"No, sir."

The answer did not really surprise him. Earlier convoys had been sent out in daring maneuvers to bring him men and supplies. But the British had crippled them all—severely.

The British controlled the island of Malta. As long as they did, it would be nearly impossible for any convoy to reach Rommel. For a moment Rommel thought about the island. On the map it was just a dot in the Mediterranean. It was in a key position between Sicily and the German-Italian bases in Libya. Only a few months before, in August of 1941, the British had launched submarines, battleships, and bombers from Malta. They had destroyed 35 percent of a convoy meant for Rommel. Most of the supplies and reinforcements had gone down. His own troops—the famed Afrika Korps—had received scarcely anything.

Above: The British, who controlled Malta, defended the island against attack by the Germans and intercepted the convoys meant for Rommel.
Below: An aerial view of Malta

A battle rages in the North African desert.

Despite the present problems, Rommel was proud of the reputation the Afrika Korps had earned in this war. Secretly, he was also proud of the nickname he had earned—the Desert Fox.

Yes, he knew the desert like a fox, and his victories had been numerous and swift. His armored tanks had lashed out across the hot sand to drive the Allies back repeatedly. His attacks had been cunning and clever—as clever as the fox for which he had been nicknamed.

But he could not work miracles. If his men weren't relieved quickly they would lose their fighting ability. They would also lose their determination. At this point, fatigue was a greater enemy than the Allies.

These German tanks and cannon were used during the North African campaign.

He also needed fuel for his great tanks. If it did not arrive soon, they would sit like so many tin locusts, rusting away beneath the glaring sun.

There had to be a way for the German High Command to stop the British raids from Malta. There simply *had* to be. If not, Rommel and his men would be isolated in this vast stretch of wasteland. For the first time, Rommel began to doubt that the British attacks could be stopped.

The destruction of the convoy in August had been bad enough. Then, in October, 63 percent of the convoy that had been sent was wiped out. Once more, on November 9, seven ships had made an attempt to reach him. They had been guarded by two 10,000-ton cruisers and ten destroyers. They had sliced through the water out across the Mediterranean. The British spotted them and attacked. Every single ship in the convoy was sunk.

Now it was December, 1941. For a moment Rommel thought about Christmas. He thought about his family back in Germany. He remembered how it was when the snow fell softly and covered the trees. He remembered how it crunched underfoot as he crossed the lawn. He thought of the Christmas tree in the window, how it looked from outside the house, its colored lights blinking. Briefly he thought of the Christmas carols. He thought of how Christmas could be if this terrible war were not going on.

Rommel, his wife, and a friend pose for a picture during happier days when they were together in France.

Quickly, Rommel pushed these thoughts aside. He had to concentrate on the British. They fought furiously. The British kept coming at him, streaming out across the desert. Their heavy artillery thudded. The hot, sultry air was filled with the thunderous roar.

The sharp crack of rifles could be heard over the din of battle. They found their targets all too often.

Rommel had been pushed all the way back to El Aghaila, the line that marked the western border. Something must be done soon, he thought. Rommel was so deep in thought that at first he did not hear the jeep. It cut across the desert, bound for the command post. It bore the swastika. As it moved, little puffs of dust curled upward. Rommel was not aware of it until it pulled up to his command post.

"General! General!" shouted a soldier. The man jumped from the jeep. Rommel looked up from the map. What could be the trouble now?

"General!" the soldier shouted. "The convoy is through! They made it past the British!"

A sudden surge of relief swept through Rommel. Yet he kept his dignity. The expression on his face was calm. He looked like a good commander who had never for a moment doubted the outcome of the battle.

The messenger handed over a packet of papers. He gave the Nazi salute smartly. Then he turned on the heel of his jack boot and made his way back toward the jeep.

Rommel opened the papers and read them with a mounting sense of joy and hope. Finally, he thought, they have gotten smart. The Germans had pulled U-boats out of the Battle of the Atlantic. They had sent them to the Mediterranean. Adolf Hitler had finally ordered more planes into the bases at Sicily.

On Christmas Eve, 1941, Rommel visited his troops in the desert somewhere between Tobruk and Sidi Omar.

If this report were accurate, the tide had turned. The Germans, he read, had attacked Malta repeatedly. The British had lost three battleships, an aircraft carrier, two cruisers, and several destroyers and submarines.

The Germans did not let up. They bombed Malta day and night. Rommel read with pleasure that the bombing had been going on for weeks. Because of this military pressure, German convoys had managed to break through. Supplies and reinforcements would reach him shortly.

Rommel smiled to himself. For sixty days he had been driven back. Now he would be able to go on the offensive again. The famed Afrika Korps would, at last, attack. He would make his plans carefully. He would carry out a well-thought-out offensive movement. Perhaps he could take the city of Tobruk. That would not be easy. But once it was done, he would be able to push on into Egypt. Rommel adjusted the papers. Yes, he thought, the British will feel the bite of the fox once more. I will be yapping at their very heels!

The information Rommel had received was correct. Sometime during the night, while the troops were sleeping and the desert was cold, the first reinforcements arrived. They reached the area eager for battle. Behind them stretched the supplies. The fuel, ammunition, and thousands of other supply items would beef up the morale and strength of the men.

When the Afrika Korps was at peak strength, Rommel attacked. He used every ounce of his talent as a great general. The thrust of his army was terrifying. The tanks and the men lashed tirelessly at the Allies.

German convoys managed to get past Malta in December of 1941. This ship reached the port of Benghazi and unloaded supplies for Rommel's troops.

The mighty Afrika Korps rolls toward the Egyptian border.

For seventeen days the mighty Afrika Korps rolled forward. They hit with such sudden force that the British reeled backward. At the end of the seventeen-day blitz, Rommel had recaptured half the ground he had lost. Still he did not stop the attack. He pushed his men onward. He urged them forward until, finally, his troops reached El Gazala. There Rommel ordered a halt.

He needed time to plan the next phase of his offensive. His men needed rest. Thinking of the terrible losses in late 1941, Rommel geared himself up for another blow at the British. Again, in May 1942, he gave the order, "Attack!"

The British were hit hard. They were forced to retreat to the Egyptian border. By June, Rommel had reached the objective he had hoped for—the city of Tobruk. His Afrika Korps came down hard on the city. For nine months Tobruk had held out. The city had withstood onslaught after onslaught. Finally, it could hold no longer against the Nazis. It fell.

By the end of June, the British saw what they had feared the most. The Desert Fox entered Egypt. The British were stunned. Rommel had pushed forward to El Alamein. He was only sixty-five miles from Alexandria and the Nile delta.

Rommel paused here, at Bardia, just short of the Egyptian border.

It seemed that nothing could stop the Fox. He stalked across the desert toward his objective. Surely one more blow would be fatal, the British told each other. In the end, they felt, Rommel would conquer Egypt. The very idea was frightening. If Rommel did that, he would then be able to sweep on northeast and capture the oil fields of the Middle East.

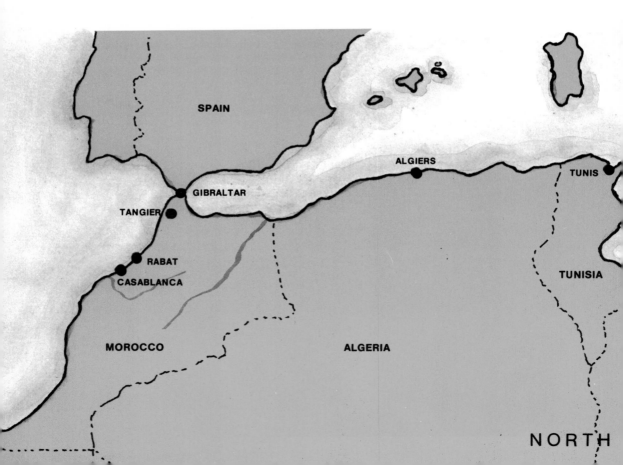

"If that happens, gentlemen," a British officer said, "the Desert Fox will push on to join the German armies in Russia."

The British watched their maps and charts and worried. Rommel, meanwhile, brought his exhausted troops to a halt at El Alamein. Tank fuel was dangerously low. It was low after every major thrust. If he hoped to go any further, another convoy of supplies must be sent to him. Hitler would have to be sure that this was done, Rommel thought.

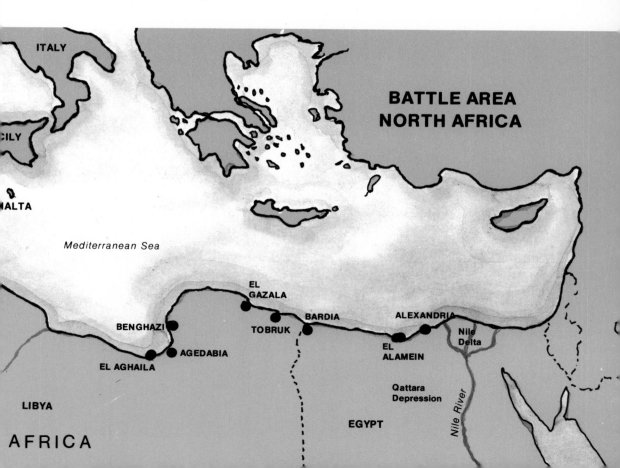

BATTLE AREA
NORTH AFRICA

ITALY

CILY

MALTA

Mediterranean Sea

EL
GAZALA

BENGHAZI

BARDIA

ALEXANDRIA

TOBRUK

Nile
Delta

AGEDABIA

EL
ALAMEIN

EL AGHAILA

LIBYA

Qattara
Depression

Nile River

EGYPT

AFRICA

Left: Hitler and Rommel
Right: A newsreel shot of
Rommel, the hero, with
two others in North Africa.

Back in Berlin, Adolf Hitler learned that
Rommel had entered Egypt. He was too delighted
to be practical. He praised the Desert Fox publicly.
He promoted Rommel to the rank of field
marshal. Hitler pounded the podium. He
proclaimed the superiority of the Nazis. His eyes
flashed. They glinted like knives over his close-
cropped black mustache. Again he made promises
to the shouting, cheering throngs of Germans.
The men on the front lines would bring victory to
the Fatherland. Hitler was carried away by his
own enthusiasm. Rommel's victories excited him.
He promised the Desert Fox that he would get
whatever he needed to continue the fight.

"Go on with your battle plans," Rommel was told. "We will see that you get what you need."

Rommel's joy was dampened by the true situation in the desert. He needed supplies. He needed men and materiel and tank fuel. He did not need a promotion. What good would a field marshal's baton do him if he had no troops to command?

Rommel pestered the German High Command. He told them over and over what he needed. He told them what he *had* to have. "I can do nothing more without these things," said Rommel.

Hitler sent word to him that he shouldn't worry. Supplies would be sent, Hitler said. Rommel believed Hitler's promise. He continued to plan his next attack. This attack would drive him closer to Alexandria. It would be launched from El Alamein.

Rommel was forced to halt his troops often because he was short of supplies. These soldiers had to sit around just waiting for fuel, materiel, and reinforcements to arrive so the desert campaign could continue.

When Hitler decided not to invade Malta, many Allied convoys were able to get through to reinforce the defenses of the island. Here, one of the incoming cruisers repels a night attack on the convoy.

Rommel did not know that Hitler didn't understand the true situation in the North African desert.

At first, Hitler planned to parachute troops onto Malta. They would secure the island. Then the Nazis could hold down the British once and for all. They could stop the British raids on the convoys headed for the Desert Fox.

Rommel knew of Hitler's plans. So he concentrated on his attack from El Alamein. He worked long and hard to make certain it did not fail.

But, suddenly, Hitler gave up the idea of invading Malta. He decided that the island could be kept quiet by the Luftwaffe. This German air force would continue its bombing raids. There was no need to parachute troops onto the island. Hitler called off the scheduled plans.

That decision was a fatal mistake for Hitler and the Nazis. It was a disaster for the Desert Fox and his Afrika Korps. In El Alamein, Rommel continued his planning. He had no way of knowing that this would be the last attack he would ever set into motion.

Finally his plans were completed. Rommel gave the order that started the awesome Afrika Korps toward Alexandria and the Nile. The tanks clanked across the scorched face of the desert. They met the British in a head-on clash of noise and fear and death.

The battle was brutal. The two armies fought along a forty-mile stretch of desert between the sea and the Qattara Depression.

"Attack!" Rommel commanded. His troops moved in. "Continue!" commanded the Desert Fox. "Keep going! Attack!"

But the Afrika Korps could not break through. On September 3 Rommel realized it was impossible to move forward. He halted the fighting and went on the defensive.

"We have no other choice for the moment," Rommel told an aide. "We must set up defensive lines."

The aide looked carefully at his commander. "Sir, are you well?"

"It is nothing!" Rommel shouted. "I gave you an order! Carry it out!"

The aide left quickly. Rommel sank into a chair. He was not well. He knew that. He had to admit to himself that he had never been this ill. Earlier that day he had been too weak to get out of his jeep. What kind of ironic fate was this? He couldn't afford to be sick. He had enough on his hands with the British. They seemed stronger than ever.

This picture was taken during the Battle of Egypt after Rommel had retreated to his own defense positions. Burning German vehicles can be seen.

Above: General Sir Harold Alexander, the commander-in-chief of the Middle East, faces the camera. Left: General Sir Bernard Law Montgomery, commander of the Eighth Army, with Air Vice Marshal H. Coningham, who is resting his foot on a captured German fuel can.

The British, stronger than ever, brought in these two new commanders to run down and trap Field Marshal Erwin Rommel, the Desert Fox.

Rommel was correct about the British. They *were* stronger than ever. They had received vast numbers of reinforcements. They had fresh men. They had new vehicles and weapons. And they had two new commanders. One was General Sir Bernard Law Montgomery, who now commanded the Eighth Army. The other was General Sir Harold Alexander, the commander-in-chief of the Middle East. These two men were determined to run down and trap the Desert Fox.

The days wore on. The Afrika Korps time and time again were kept from advancing. Then Rommel's illness grew worse. Finally, he was forced to make a decision he had hoped he would never have to make. He had to go on sick leave. Through all his years as a soldier and commander, Rommel had been sent behind the lines to hospitals only when he was wounded. But now he was forced to return. The infection had weakened him and drained him of his strength.

The hospital bed in Berlin was far from the steaming desert and the chaos of battle. Rommel lay there. He tried to rest. He wondered how General Stumme was doing. Stumme was acting as his replacement until he recovered. He wondered if the battle had changed. Maybe his Afrika Korps was on the offensive again. As soon as he was well—

Suddenly his bedside telephone rang. He ignored the ring. He was still too weak to take calls. He needed rest. But the phone was persistent. Rommel finally picked up the receiver.

He heard a familiar voice on the other end of the line. It was Adolf Hitler. Hitler told him things

Rommel, back on the job in North Africa, quenches his thirst.

were going badly in Africa. Nobody, said Hitler, seemed to know where General Stumme was. "Will you go back?" Hitler asked the Desert Fox.

"Of course," Rommel replied.

Exhausted and sick, Rommel pulled himself out of the hospital bed. He was puzzled over the disappearance of General Stumme. Where could he be? It made no sense at all.

Rommel had a tiring journey. He was back at his command post in the desert by the following evening. His aide briefed him on what had been going on. Although weak, Rommel listened carefully. As he listened, he began to dread the worst. Somehow he knew that the battle had already been lost.

Rommel congratulates Lieutenant-General Ludwig Cruewell on his birthday, March 20, 1942. Cruewell had taken over command of the Afrika Korps after Rommel's promotion to Field Marshal.

"And General Stumme?" he finally asked. "Where is he? A commander does not simply disappear."

"He went out with a driver, sir," answered the aide. "That was the last time he was seen."

"Find out what happened," commanded Rommel. "I want a full report as soon as possible."

Rommel received his report. It confirmed that General Stumme had, indeed, gone out with the driver. They had come under British attack. The driver had turned around sharply. He had headed back to safe territory. Apparently, General Stumme had fallen out of the vehicle. He started to run. The attacking British chased him. Stumme suffered a heart attack. He died where he fell.

Rommel was dismayed at the turn of events. He tossed the report aside. The whole incident was absurd. Certainly any man could die of fright. But to fall out of a jeep? Rommel was irritated.

Even worse news reached Rommel on November 2. General Montgomery had broken through the lines on the southern sector of the front. The Italian divisions, under Rommel's command, were positioned there. They were supposed to hold the line. They weren't able to. Montgomery had overrun them.

Reports from the southern sector streamed in. Rommel read each one with rising anxiety. Finally, he radioed Hitler. "I can't hold out," he said. "There simply is no way. I intend to withdraw while there is still a chance. I can make it to the Fuka position if I withdraw quickly."

RAF Hurricane II fighter planes over Egypt

Fuka was forty miles to the west. Rommel did not wait for official approval. He ordered his men to pull back.

Rommel organized each phase of the withdrawal. He was trying desperately to pull the Afrika Korps back from the vicious British attack. In the midst of the retreat, he received a long message from Hitler.

Rommel read the long, wordy order. He slowly realized that Hitler was telling him not to retreat, not "one step." Rommel was horrified. He could not believe his eyes. Yet there it was. "You can show your troops no other way," said Hitler, "than that which leads to victory or to death."

What was this nonsense? Rommel slammed the message down on his table. That is crazy, he thought. The man doesn't know what he's asking me to do!

Rommel paced back and forth. He felt totally helpless. He did not know what to do. No—that was not true. He knew exactly what he must do. He had to continue the withdrawal he had already begun.

Yet here was a direct order from Adolf Hitler himself. Rommel was not to give up one inch of the desert—not one inch.

British armored vehicles advance in the desert.

Rommel and his staff in western Egypt.

At last, Rommel stopped pacing. His face was drawn. He had an enormous responsibility to his men, to his country, and to Hitler. Hitler had given a direct order. Rommel was a responsible field marshal. He was a responsible German soldier. He could not refuse that order. Obedience and discipline were necessary to the entire Nazi system. Without them it would break down. Without them the powerful Nazi war machine would come to a halt.

I must obey, thought Rommel. I cannot do anything else. Perhaps I can make Hitler understand the position we are in. Yes, that's it. Perhaps I can persuade him to approve the retreat.

Rommel knew that was the only answer. In the meantime, he could not disobey Hitler. That would make him guilty of treason. For the moment, Rommel had to obey Hitler's order.

"Halt the withdrawal!" Rommel commanded. "Tell the troops to stand fast!"

Even as he spoke, Rommel knew it was the wrong thing to do. They couldn't delay much longer. If they did, the Afrika Korps would be totally destroyed by Montgomery and the British army. Reluctantly, Rommel repeated his command. "Halt the withdrawal."

Then he said, "Send a courier to me at once!" When the courier arrived, Rommel briefed him quickly. The courier must make his way to Hitler as soon as possible. He must tell Hitler how desperate was the situation on the battlefront. He must explain to him that withdrawal of the troops was the only way to save them. Once he understands, Rommel thought, he will permit me to save my men.

The courier saluted and left quietly.

Rommel waited. He was impatient. It would take awhile for the courier to deliver his message. But he was certain that Hitler would permit him to draw the troops back. He would have to once he realized what Rommel was up against. Wouldn't he? Rommel waited.

But the British did not wait. The sound of heavy artillery shattered the desert air. The heavy shells screamed. Their aim was deadly. Explosions shook the earth. The roar of destruction was deafening. Men fought bravely, and died. The cry for "Medic!" was heard along the desert as Afrika Korps troops tried to help their fallen comrades.

One of the many Germans and Italians wounded during the desert battle.

Rommel (above) looks concerned,
as some of his men (right)
discuss the unhappy situation.

And still Montgomery's forces came. They drove forward. They knew they had the Nazis on the run. They, too, had known what it was like to retreat. Now it was their turn at victory. The very knowledge that the Desert Fox was fleeing spurred the British on to even greater effort. And on they came. The guns roared. The mortars whined. The rifles cracked.

The reports continued to come back from the front. Rommel sat helplessly at his table. He agonized over the useless loss of life. He had never known such frustration—not in his entire military career. Things had never been this bad. Never had so many men died so needlessly. Hitler was forcing Rommel to sit back and watch the slaughter of the Afrika Korps. If the withdrawal had been permitted to continue, many of the troops would now be alive.

Still Rommel waited for an answer from Hitler.

But the British had no intention of waiting for anything. They unleashed all the destructive power that was at their disposal. They swept down on the Germans with terrifying momentum. Montgomery's forces could not be stopped.

Rommel looked at his calendar. It was November 4, 1942. He locked the date in his mind. What he was about to do could get him court-martialed. He was about to disobey an order. Worse, he was about to disobey a direct order from Adolf Hitler.

But this was a time when human decency was more important than the order of a superior. Rommel could no longer stand by and watch his men die senselessly. This order was madness. He would no longer tolerate it—regardless of the consequences.

"Tell the troops to withdraw!" Rommel orderd.

"Sir?" The aide looked doubtful. No word had yet arrived from Hitler.

"I said to retreat!" shouted Rommel. "That's an order!"

"Yes, sir!"

The word spread quickly down the line. German troops, firing at the British, heard the command as it was passed along. Italian troops, fighting desperately, heard the order.

Camels in North Africa as seen from a German plane over the desert

It was the only order that had made any sense to them since the fierce battle had begun. El Alamein seemed only a place in a dream now. The mighty Afrika Korps, led by their world-famous leader, Field Marshal Erwin Rommel—the Desert Fox—hightailed it toward Fuka.

The attacking British came after them. They overtook the fleeing men. More and more Afrika Korps troops fell under the mighty onslaught.

Italian tank abandoned in the desert for lack of fuel

Rommel led his men to Fuka. But he soon realized that General Montgomery had no intention of stopping there. If Rommel did not continue to retreat, his army would be wiped out. There would no longer be an Afrika Korps.

The Desert Fox pulled back even farther. The next day the courier found Rommel. Hitler officially approved the retreat.

Rommel shook his head. It was too little too late. Had he not stopped the withdrawal, perhaps many of the men could have been saved. Now—when all was nearly over—Hitler approved what Rommel had known was correct from the beginning.

But now there was no longer any hope of regrouping the troops. Now it was impossible to launch an attack against Montgomery. Rommel had nothing left to fight with. Montgomery had overrun Fuka. Rommel had no place to stop.

Above: A wrecked Italian plane found near Tobruk on February 17, 1943
Below: This 150 mm assault gun mounted on a self-propelled tank was
left behind by the Afrika Korps. Though undamaged, the tank had
run out of fuel.

He did the only thing left for him to do. He continued the retreat. He forced his exhausted men farther and farther from Fuka. For fifteen days he retreated. He retreated more than seven hundred miles—beyond Benghazi.

At the end of the long, bitter trek, Rommel stopped. He looked out over what was left of one of the greatest fighting forces of the war. The Afrika Korps had been destroyed. Nothing was left except 25,000 Italians, 10,000 Germans, and 60 tanks.

The Desert Fox had been beaten. And with the fall of the fox began the fall of Adolf Hitler and the destruction of Nazi Germany.

General Crawford, Colonel Gruver, and Corporal Brooks have dinner on the desert near Tobruk on March 13, 1943, after the Afrika Korps had retreated.

Field Marshal Erwin Rommel

# INDEX

*Page numbers in boldface type
indicate illustrations*

*About the Author*

A native of Alabama, G.C. Skipper has traveled throughout the world, including Jamaica, Haiti, India, Argentina, the Bahamas, and Mexico. He has written several other children's books as well as an adult novel. Mr. Skipper has also published numerous articles in national magazines. He is now working on his second adult novel. Mr. Skipper and his family live in North Wales, Pennsylvania, a suburb of Philadelphia.